That Palace in Washington

An Anecdotal History
of
White House Entertaining
1800 - 1850

Patricia B. Mitchell

Sarah E. Mitchell, Editor

With Bibliographical Notes

Published 2004 by the author at Mitchells Publications, P. O. Box 429, Chatham, VA 24531.
Telephone/fax: 434-432-0595
Book Sales: 800-967-2867
E-mail: answers@foodhistory.com
Website: www.foodhistory.com

Printed in the U. S. A.
ISBN 1-929384-01-7

- Illustrations -

Front Cover - "President's House" (as seen from the southwest), engraving by George Lehman, provided by the Library of Congress.

Inside Title Page - "The Great Cheese Levee" of 1837 (see description on page 20 of this book), from Ben Perley Poore, **Perley's Reminiscences of Sixty Years in the National Metropolis, Vol. I**, Hubbard Brothers, Philadelphia, 1886.

Inside Back Cover - portrait of the author by David L. Mitchell.

Back Cover - "View of the President's House" (from the north), engraving by D. W. Kellogg & Co., Hartford, provided by the Library of Congress.

Table of Contents

Introduction

The President's dining habits have always been of interest to the public. What does the Commander-in-Chief like to eat? Are he and his wife extravagant in their tastes and expenditures, or modest? How does the First Family entertain?

The purpose of this book (and its subsequent companion volumes) is to tell a little about the history of the White House and its culinary department, and to shed some light on the dietary preferences and quirks of some of the presidents and their families.

We begin with an overview of the origins of the capital city and the Executive Mansion.

"Recipe" for a Seat of Government: Washington Administration April 30, 1789 - March 3, 1797

In 1790, George Washington was authorized by Congress "to appoint commissioners to survey, under his own direction, a district of territory, not exceeding ten miles square, at some place on the River Potomac . . ." [1] near Georgetown, Virginia.[2] This area of land would become Washington, D. C. Major Charles Pierre L'Enfant, a French engineer who had served in the Revolution, was hired to be the city planner, and Andrew Ellicott was engaged to be surveyor and assistant to L'Enfant.[3] George Washington and Major L'Enfant together chose the site for the White House.[4]

A contest, with a $500 prize, was held for the best plan for the residence of the Chief Executive.[5] (Thomas Jefferson himself may have pseudonymously submitted a drawing.[6]) An architect in Charleston, South Carolina, James Hoban, was one of the men to submit an architectural plan. Hoban had designed many buildings in his home state, including private residences and the South Carolina State House at Columbia.[7]

Hoban's design won the contest, which was judged by the city commissioners. Hoban, who was a native of Dublin, Ireland, reportedly said that he based the design for the White House on the Duke of Leinster's mansion in Dublin.[8] Others note that the U. S. "President's House" resembles a smaller version of Chatsworth House, Derbyshire, England,[9] or other European homes or buildings.

In July 1792 the commissioners of the Federal City asked Hoban to supervise the construction of his building (minus its porches and wings and one story,[10] in order to keep down the cost[11]), and on October 13, 1792 the cornerstone was laid.[12]

Almost eight years elapsed between the time that Hoban won the contest and the first occupancy of the White House. As a result, Martha and George Washington never lived in the White House, their executive residences having been located in New York City (1789-1790) and Philadelphia (1790-1797).

John Adams Administration
March 4, 1797 - March 3, 1801

When John and Abigail Adams moved from Philadelphia to Washington, D. C., and into the White House in 1800, not a single apartment was finished and only six rooms were livable.[13] Plaster throughout the mansion was still damp, call bells for the thirty servants had not been installed; construction of the principal staircases had not been completed (and was not expected to be finished that winter); and over half of Mrs. Adams' tea china had been broken or stolen in transit from Philadelphia.[14]

In the autumn of 1800 Mrs. Adams wrote to her daughter that: "The lighting [of] the apartments, from the kitchen to parlors and chambers, is a tax indeed . . . . [I]f they will . . . let me have wood enough to keep fires, I design to be pleased." [15] For lack of a better place, the laundry was hung in the now-grand East Room.[16]

Despite the drawbacks of her new home, Mrs. Adams advised her daughter, "It is a beautiful spot, capable of every improvement, and the more I view it, the more I am delighted with it." [17]

On January 1, 1801, the president's home was officially opened to the public. After President Adams and his wife greeted the guests in the oval room upstairs,[18] refreshments were served. Coffee, tea, punch, wine, syllabub, Floating Island, trifles, curds, creams, and jellies accompanied cakes and tarts.[19]

When dining alone, the President, Abigail, and their granddaughter Susanna, who lived with them, frequently enjoyed lunches of lemonade and oat-cakes.[20]

These repasts were prepared in the ground floor kitchen, which resembled the kitchen of a hotel or a large family estate. Architect James Hoban positioned the kitchen in the middle of the basement floor on the north side of the "President's House," as it was known. (The President's House was called the White House as early as 1812, but the name did not become official until Theodore Roosevelt's term.[21]) The kitchen featured two vast stone fireplaces for cooking and barred windows to admit natural light from the north.[22] (Incidentally, the basement is actually the ground floor if viewed from the river, or south, side of the building.[23])

Ike Hoover, who was part of the White House staff for forty-two years, wrote about the old kitchen as it looked in 1891. At the time it was being used as an "engine room" (or boiler and furnace room):

> *"In the kitchen of the original house . . . could be seen the old open fireplaces once used for broiling the chickens and baking the hoecakes for the early Fathers of our country, the old cranes and spits still in place. Out of the door to the rear there yet remained the old winevault, the meathouse, and the smokehouse. So vivid were these reminders you could still almost smell the wine odors and the aroma from the hams and bacon that must have been so deliciously and painstakingly prepared here. . . ."* [24]

In the early kitchen an annual coat of whitewash lightened smoke- and grease-stained walls.[25] The floor of brick pavers was sprinkled with clean creek sand to soak up moisture and grease.[26] Adjacent to the kitchen were pantries and storage compartments for food, equipment, and serving ware.[27]

Because the Adams couple lived in the White House only a few months, they did not give many parties while there. However, the following recipes are representative of the sort which they might have served at a reception:

Orgeat,

A Necessary Refreshment at all Parties

"Boil two quarts of milk with a stick of cinnamon and let it stand to be quite cold, first taking out the cinnamon; blanch four ounces of the best sweet almonds, pound them in a marble mortar with a little rose-water; mix them well with the milk, sweeten it to your taste, and let it boil a few minutes only, lest the almonds should be oily; strain it through a very fine sieve till quite smooth, and free from the almonds, serve it up either cold or lukewarm, in glasses with handles." [28]

Raspberry Cream

"Take a quart of thick sweet cream and boil it two or three wallops, then take it off the fire and strain some juices of raspberries into it to your taste, stir it a good while before you put your juice in, that it may be almost cold, when you put it to it, and afterwards stir it one way for almost a quarter of an hour; then sweeten it to your taste and when it is cold you may send it up." [29]

Note: Wallops are the series of noisy, bubbling motions made by water or other liquids reaching the boiling point or boiling rapidly. In cooking, one such bubbling action was used as a vague measure of time.

Jefferson Administration
March 4, 1801 - March 3, 1809

Thomas Jefferson, the third president, asked one of his two adult daughters or Dolley Madison, wife of his Secretary of State, to act as official White House hostess, since Jefferson's wife had died nineteen years before he became president.

Jefferson did not immediately move into the White House after his inauguration because "'The Palace,' as the President's House was dubbed satirically, was not yet finished; its walls were not fully plastered, and it still lacked the main staircase – which, it must be admitted, was a serious defect." [30]

Jefferson, a man most knowledgeable about, and appreciative of, fine foods and wine, employed a French chef, Honoré Julien, in the White House.[31] His mâitre d' hôtel was Etienne Lemaire, who "had served some of the best families abroad." [32] Jefferson also brought Annette, a slave from Monticello, to the President's House, for she knew just how to prepare batter cakes, hot breads, fried apples, eggs, and bacon for Jefferson's breakfasts.[33] However, Jefferson generally preferred French cooking because "the meats [were] more tender." [34]

It is reported that the President spent $20,000 on wines and brandies during his eight years as Chief of State.[35] Senator Plumer of New Hampshire wrote,"We sat down at the table at four, rose at six, and walked immediately into another room and drank coffee. We had a very good dinner, with a profusion of fruits and sweetmeats. The wine was the best I ever drank, particularly the champagne, which was indeed delicious." [36]

Jefferson turned his innovative mind toward making entertaining in the Executive Mansion dining room more private, in order that affairs of state could be discussed. He had a set of circular shelves installed in a wall of the dining room. Upon touching a spring these shelves would revolve into the room, Lazy Susan-style, filled with food placed on them by servants in the adjoining room. When entertaining people with which he wished to enjoy private conversation, Jefferson limited the number of guests to four and had a diminutive tiered table with rotating shelves (called a dumbwaiter, as was the device just described), placed beside each diner, so that no servants at all needed to be on hand.[37]

When President John F. Kennedy entertained a group of Nobel laureates at a White House dinner, he remarked, "I believe this is the most extraordinary collection of talent, of human knowledge, that has ever been gathered together at the White House, with the possible exception of when Thomas Jefferson dined alone." [38]

Jefferson was fond of soup, admired French culture, and loved green peas, so the following soup would probably have pleased him:

French Green Pea Soup

"This soup is made without meat. Put into a soup-pot four quarts of shelled green peas, two large onions sliced, a handful of leaves of sweet marjoram shred from the stalks, or a handful of sweet basil; or a mixed handful of both — also, if you like it, a handful of green mint. Add four quarts of water, and boil the whole slowly till all the peas are entirely to pieces. Then take off the pot, and mash the peas well against its sides to extract from them all their flavour. Afterward strain off the liquid into a clean pot, and add to it a tea-cup full of the juice of spinach, which you must prepare, while the soup is boiling, by pounding some spinach in a mortar. This will give the soup a fine green colour. Then put in a quarter of a pound of the best fresh butter rolled whole in flour; and add a pint and a half more of shelled young peas. If you wish the soup very thick, you may allow a quart of the additional peas. Season it with a very little salt and cayenne; put it again over the fire, and boil it till the last peas are quite soft, but not till they go to pieces.

"Have ready in a tureen two or three slices of toasted bread cut into small squares or dice, and pour the

soup on it . . . . What is left may be warmed for the next day." [39]

Perhaps Annette prepared batter cakes like these:

Batter Cakes

"Boil two cups of small homony [hominy grits] very soft; add an equal quantity of corn meal with a little salt, and a large spoonful of butter; make it in[to] a thin batter with three eggs, and a sufficient quantity of milk — beat all together some time, and bake them on a griddle, or in woffle [sic] irons. When eggs cannot be procured, yeast makes a good substitute; put a spoonful in the batter, and let it stand an hour to rise." [40]

Madison Administration
March 4, 1809 - March 3, 1817

James and Dolley Madison moved into the White House next. Dolley was experienced in the role of White House hostess because, as already mentioned, she had often acted in that capacity for the widower President Jefferson.

Speaking of whom, Jefferson paid Dolley the compliment of attending the first inaugural ball (a custom which Dolley instituted). Ex-president Jefferson confessed that it had been more than forty years since he had been to a ball. [41]

Dolley was a most charming hostess. It was said that, "During her reign, people went there not only because it was the President's house, but because it was socially the most delightful place in the world. She was merry, intellectual and generous." Washington Irving described her: "Mrs. Madison is a fine, portly, buxom dame, who has a smile and a pleasant word for everyone." [42] Dolley made it a practice to serve refreshments to all guests, whatever the purpose or length of their visit. During the first year of her husband's tenure, she pleased and surprised the British minister by sending in glasses of punch and seed cake as he conferred with President Madison.[43]

At her husband's second inauguration banquet in 1812, Dolley served a "trendy" dessert, helping to popularize it. A quote from the time says,

> *"Mrs. Madison always entertains brilliantly, but last night there was a sparkle in her eye that set astir an air of expectancy in her guests. . . . When finally the brilliant assemblage, America's best, entered the dining room, they beheld in the center, high on a silver platter, a large shining dome of pink ice cream." [44]*

Ice cream had been known for centuries, but because of the problem of obtaining ice and keeping it frozen, ice cream was a rare treat, even among the wealthy. After the ice box was patented in 1803, and other technological advances were made, the delicacy became more available.

A contemporary account of entertaining during "Dolley days" reads this way:

> *"The President, or rather his lady, holds a drawing-room weekly, during the sitting of Congress. He takes by the hand those who are presented to him; shaking hands being discovered in America to be more rational and manly than kissing them. For the rest, it is much as such things are every where, chatting, and tea, compliments and ices, a little music, (Some scandal, I suppose, among the ladies,) and to bed." [45]*

Dolley, by all accounts, set a lavish table. She delighted in serving a panoply of dishes at each meal. When she was criticized for the variety of food and generous servings by a foreign visitor, who said "that it was more like a harvest-home supper, than the entertainment of a Secretary of State," she responded that "[I] thought abundance was preferable to elegance; that circumstances formed customs, and customs formed taste; and as the profusion so repugnant to foreign customs arose from the happy circumstance of the superabundance and prosperity of our country, [I] did not hesitate to sacrifice the delicacy of European taste for the less elegant, but more liberal fashion of Virginia." [46]

The happy entertaining was interrupted by the War of 1812. In fact, a particular meal was somewhat disrupted by the advancing British forces. On August 24, 1814, Dolley told the slave Paul Jennings to prepare the table for 40 guests, since she was expecting the President and victorious officers to return to the White House after defeating the English. Jennings proceeded with meal preparations, but suddenly a messenger arrived, telling them to evacuate the White House, for there had been a dreadful American defeat at the Battle of Bladensburg.[47]

Dolley kept her wits about her, and instructed that the Gilbert Stuart portrait of George Washington should be quickly removed from its frame and be handed over to two gentleman who would spirit it away for safekeeping. Dolley also gathered "as many Cabinet papers into trunks as to fill one carriage," [48] including a draft of the Declaration of Independence, all of which were saved.[49]

Around 9 p.m. that night, British seamen stormed the White House. However, before the English arrived the fleeing American militiamen "had presence of mind enough to save a large quantity of the wine by drinking it." [50] (Dolley and her entourage were long gone.) The English officers ate the dinner and, with the left-behind wine, made a toast to President Madison, "for being such a good fellow as to leave us such a capitol supper." [51]

One of the sailors took the Madisons' small wooden medicine chest. 125 years later it was returned by a Canadian who was a descendant of that British "souvenir hunter." The medicinal herbs the chest contained were still recognizable.[52]

Back to the past: After eating dinner, the British set fire to the White House, gutting it. (The White House was not open to the public again until 1818.) During the remainder of the

Madison administration, James and Dolley lived successively at two other Washington residences. When James Monroe became president, the Madisons retired to Montpelier, their home in Virginia, where they continued to entertain in fine style. After Mr. Madison's death, Dolley moved back to Washington, where she was still extremely popular. However, before Congress purchased her husband's papers when she was about eighty, her finances became depleted.[53] Her former servant, Paul Jennings, was often sent by Daniel Webster, his employer, "with a market basket of provisions" for Dolley. Mr. Webster also directed Jennings to take her "anything in the house that I thought she was in need of." Jennings added that he "often did this, and occasionally gave her small sums from my own pocket, though I had years before bought my freedom of her." [54]

A recipe similar to the following might have been enjoyed in the Madison White House, though fresh tomatoes would more likely have been used, rather than canned:

Bouillon á la James Madison

"Two gallons of water, put in several bones — ham bones are excellent — three good[-]sized carrots, three onions, celery, a can of tomatoes, salt and pepper to taste. Simmer, covered closely, all day and night. Strain into a large bowl. When cold remove grease carefully. Cut like dice three pounds of rump of beef, break two eggs over this meat, add celery, salt and pepper and add the bouillon to it; put on the fire and stir until the froth rises. Skim carefully, strain through a flannel and set aside for use. When ready to serve, heat and add a glass of good sherry." [55]

Two recipes follow, one for "an ordinary Seed-Cake," the other for "a rich Seed Cake." One might surmise that Dolley would have preferred the latter.

To make an ordinary Seed-Cake

*"Take six pounds of fine flour, rub it into a thimble-full
of carraway-seeds [sic] finely beaten, and two nutmegs
grated, and mace beaten; then heat a quart of cream hot
enough to melt a pound of butter in it, and when it is no
more than blood-warm, mix your cream and butter with
a pint of good ale yeast, and then wet your flour with it;
make it pretty thin; just before it goes in the oven, put in
a pound of rough carraways [sic], and some citron sliced
thin; three quarters of an hour in a quick oven will bake
it."* [56]

A rich Seed Cake, call'd the Nun's Cake

*"Take four pounds of your finest flour, and three
pounds of double refined sugar beaten and sifted, mix
them together, and dry them by the fire till you prepare
your other materials. Take four pounds of butter, beat it
in your hands till it is very soft like cream, then beat
thirty five eggs, leave out sixteen whites, and strain out
the treddles [yolks] of the rest, and beat them and the
butter together till all appears like butter; put in four or
five spoonfuls of rose or orange-flower water, and beat
it again; then take your flour and sugar, with six ounces
of carraway-seeds [sic], and strew it in by degrees,
beating it up all the time for two hours together; you may
put in as much tincture of cinnamon or ambergrease
[ambergris] as you please; butter your hoop, and let it
stand three hours in a moderate oven."* [57]

The next dish could have found its place amidst "the
profusion of [Dolley's] table:"

Chicken Pudding,
A Favourite Virginia Dish

*"Beat ten eggs very light, add to them a quart of rich
milk, with a quarter of a pound of butter melted, and*

*some pepper and salt; stir in as much flour as will make
a thin good batter; take four young chickens, and after
cleaning them nicely, cut off the legs, wings, &c. put
them all in a sauce pan, with some salt and water, and a
bundle of thyme and parsley, boil them till nearly done,
then take the chicken from the water and put it in the
batter[,] pour it in a deep dish, and bake it; send nice
white gravy in a boat [to the table with it]."* [58]

Monroe Administration
March 4, 1817 - March 3, 1825

Elegance reigned in the "resurrected" White House of the
Monroe years. Even if Mrs. Monroe did not light up a room like
a thousand candles as Mrs. Madison had, she spent $100 a night
on candles to light the East Room, and her guests dined on the
creations of a French chef.[59] (The Monroes were much
influenced by European culture, for James Monroe had served as
Minister to France, England, and Spain.)

James Fenimore Cooper described a visit to the White
House:

*"The dining-room was in better taste than is common
here, being quite simple and but little furnished. The
table was large and rather handsome. The service was
in china, as is uniformly the case. . . . There was,
however, a rich plateau, and a great abundance of the
smaller articles of table-plate. The cloth, napkins, &c.,
&c., were fine and beautiful.*

*"The dinner was served in the French style, a little
Americanized. The dishes were handed around, though
some of the guests, appearing to prefer their own
customs, coolly helped themselves to what they found at
hand.*

"Of attendants there were a good many. They were neatly dressed, out of livery, and sufficient. To conclude, the whole entertainment might have passed for a better sort of European dinner-party, at which the guests were too numerous for general or very agreeable discourse, and some of them too new to be entirely at their ease.

"Mrs. Monroe arose at the end of the dessert, and withdrew, attended by two or three of the most gallant of the company. No sooner was his wife's back turned than the President reseated himself, inviting his guests to imitate the action. After allowing his guests sufficient time to renew . . . he arose himself, giving the hint to his company, that it was time to rejoin the ladies. In the drawing-room coffee was served, and every one [sic] left the house before nine." [60]

Mrs. Monroe frequently gave evening "drawing rooms." According to a newspaper of the time, these weekly receptions were attended by "secretaries, senators, foreign Ministers, consuls, auditors, accountants, officers of the Army and Navy of every grade, . . . farmers, merchants, parsons, priests, lawyers, judges, auctioneers, and nothingarians, all with their wives, and some with their gawky offspring; some in shoes, most in boots, and many in spurs; some snuffing, others chewing and many longing for their cigars and whiskey punch at home." [61]

One of the notable events of the Monroe tenure was the wedding of the Monroe's younger daughter Maria. Seventeen-year-old Maria married her cousin, Samuel L. Gouverneur of New York, one of her father's secretaries. The East Room nuptials were very exclusive and only family and a few friends were invited, but a drawing-room was held a few days after the wedding to allow society to "pay its respects" to the bride. [62]

Another glittery event at the White House was a visit by the beloved Marquis de Lafayette at the end of the Monroe administration. [63]

During the Monroe's sojourn, the White House was furnished with gracefully beautiful French furniture, including a marble-top table and a pier table that are the only two pieces of furniture which have remained continuously in the White House since 1817. A magnificent seven-piece silver dining table centerpiece of the Monroe era is still a treasured White House possession.[64] This bronze-doré mirrored plateau or *surtout de table*, when extended to its full length, is thirteen and a half feet long and two feet wide. A low bronze rim surrounds the flat surface of mirrors. The rim is decorated with small garlands of vines and fruits. At equidistant intervals along the rim are removable figures of Bacchus and Bacchantes holding up crowns for candles and crystal vases for flowers.[65] At the same time the Monroes ordered the plateau at a cost of $1,200, they purchased matching candelabra, fruit epergnes, and vases.[66] A purchase totaling $94 for "kitchen utensils" is also recorded.[67]

A dish similar to this might have graced the Monroe dining table:

French Chicken Salad

"Take a large, fine, cold [cooked] fowl, and having removed the skin and fat, cut the flesh from the bones in very small shreds, not more than an inch long. The dressing should not be made till immediately before it goes to table. Have ready half a dozen or more hard-boiled eggs. Cut up the yolks upon a plate, and with the back of a wooden spoon mash them to a paste, adding a small salt-spoonful of salt, rather more of cayenne pepper, and a large teaspoonful of made mustard. Mix them well together; then add two large table-spoonfuls of salad oil, and one of the best cider vinegar. All these ingredients for the dressing must be mixed to a fine, smooth, stiff, yellow paste. Lay the [shredded] chicken in a nice even heap, upon the middle of a flat dish, smoothing it, and making it circular or oval with the back of a spoon, and flattening the top. Then cover it thickly and smoothly with the dressing, or paste of seasoned yolk of egg, &c. Have ready a large head of lettuce that has been picked, and washed in cold water;

and, cutting up the best parts of it very small, mix the lettuce with a portion of the hard-boiled white of egg minced fine. Lay the chopped lettuce all round the heap of [shredded] chicken, &c. Then ornament the surface with very small bits of boiled red beets, and green pickled cucumbers, cut into slips and dots, and arranged in a pretty pattern upon the yellow ground of the coating that covers the chicken. After taking on your plate a portion of each part of the salad, mix all together before eating it." [68]

The following classic dish, with a texture more like pudding than typical bread, would have been a welcomed sight to 19th-century diners.

Virginia Spoon Bread

"Put one quart of milk on the fire and when it comes to a boil, stir in four tablespoons of white corn meal. Let it cook until very thick, stirring constantly. Put it aside to cool. Then add three eggs which have been beaten, two tablespoons of flour and a big pinch of salt. Beat in one tablespoon of butter while the mixture is hot. Bake in a buttered dish for thirty-five minutes and serve immediately." [69]

John Quincy Adams Administration
March 4, 1825 - March 3, 1829

Of the first six presidents, only two were not Virginians — John Quincy Adams and his father, John Adams (the second president), who were from Massachusetts. Personal philosophy, however, guided each president more than regional differences. For example, George Washington expected that great pomp and formality be demonstrated in affairs of state. He was aware of the ceremonies and forms of French and English courts, and received visitors dressed magnificently, his sword at his side.[70] At Mrs. Washington's receptions, she "received precisely after the manner of Queen Charlotte's drawing-room levees. The guests were arranged standing against the walls, and the President's wife marched the rounds and said a kind word to all." [71] Washington's successor, John Adams, who had spent some years in France and England, followed the ceremonial forms adopted by Washington, but the third president, Thomas Jefferson, was more "egalitarian" in his lifestyle, doing away with formality whenever possible, and behaving more like an ordinary "citozen." (Jefferson was of kindred spirit with the French Revolutionists.[72]) John Quincy Adams, similarly to his father, appreciated grandeur, for John Quincy had grown up in European society, and was influenced by his parents' thinking.[73]

John Quincy Adams, like most presidents, had a long public career prior to becoming president. He had served as a diplomat and Secretary of State under President Monroe. He and his wife were socially skilled. Mrs. Adams held the usual evening levees and reportedly improved the quality of refreshments served.[74] Dinners were prepared by the French chef Michael Anthony Guista. A description of one state dinner tells of forty covers (place settings) and an atmosphere "very splendid and rather stiff," [75] although, according to one writer, Mrs. J. Q. Adams achieved a pleasing balance between the constrained formality of the "drawing-rooms" of her mother-in-law Mrs. John Adams and the laissez-faire mood of receptions given by President Jefferson's daughters.[76]

Chef Guista prepared Continental cuisine and also dished up New England favorites for the First Family. Here is a rather labor-intensive soup recipe, the likes of which the chef might have prepared for the Adams:

The Best Clam Soup

"Put fifty clams into a large pot of boiling water, to make the shells open easily. [Set aside.] Take a knuckle of veal, cut it into pieces (four calves' feet split in half will be still better) and put it into a soup-pot with the

liquor of the clams, and a quart of rich milk, or cream, adding a large bunch of sweet ma[r]joram, and a few leaves of sage, cut into pieces, and a head of celery chopped small; also, a dozen whole pepper-corns, but no salt, as the salt[i]ness of the clam liquor will be sufficient. Boil it till all the meat of the veal drops from the bones, then strain off the soup and return it to the pot, which must first be washed out. Having in the meantime cut up the clams, and pounded them in a mortar, (which will cause them to flavour the soup much better,) season them with two dozen blades of mace, and two powdered nutmegs; mix with them a quarter of a pound of fresh butter, and put them into the soup with all the liquor that remains about them. After the clams are in, let it boil another quarter of an hour. Have ready some thick slices of nicely-toasted bread, (with the crust removed,) cut them into small square mouthfuls; put them into a tureen; and pour the soup upon them. It will be found excellent. Oyster soup may be made in the same manner." [77]

This robust flavor of the following fruity pudding and its stick-to-the-ribs texture would insure that no one left the table with an un-stuffed stomach.

Boston Pudding

"Make a good common paste with a pound and a half of flour, and three quarters of a pound of butter. (Or three quarters of a pound of beef suet, chopped very fine. Mix the suet at once with the flour, knead it with cold water into a stiff dough, and then roll it out into a large thin sheet. Fold it up and roll it again.) When you roll it out the last time, cut off the edges, till you get the sheet of paste . . . an even square shape.

"Have ready some fruit sweetened to your taste. If cranberries, gooseberries, dried peaches, or damsons, they should be stewed, and made very sweet. If apples, they should be stewed in a very little water, drained, and

seasoned with nutmeg, rose-water and lemon. If currants, raspberries, or blackberries, they should be mashed with sugar, and put into the pudding raw.

"Spread the fruit very thick, all over the sheet of paste, (which must not be rolled out too thin.) When it is covered all over with the fruit, roll it up, and close the dough at both ends, and down the last side. Tie the pudding in a cloth and boil it three hours.

"Eat it with sugar. It must not be taken out of the pot till just before it is brought to table." [78]

Jackson Administration
March 4, 1829 - March 3, 1837

Jackson attempted to be a "direct representative of the common man," trying to "democratize" Washington.[79] His lovely and hospitable home, the Hermitage near Nashville, Tennessee, however, discounts any image of an uncouth frontiersman. The popular politician and 1812 war hero enjoyed the Hermitage with his beloved wife Rachel. She, unfortunately, did not live to reside with him in the White House. In a sad, self-fulfilling prophecy Rachel had exclaimed, when presented with the idea of dwelling in the White House, "I assure you that I would rather be a doorkeeper in the house of God, than to live in that Palace in Washington!" [80]

Following Jackson's 1829 inauguration the portals of the White House were thrown open for the general populace. People entered the White House through doors and windows and packed the building. In the crowded reception areas, "waiters emerging from doors with loaded trays were borne to the floor by the crush; china and glassware were smashed; gallons of punch were spilled on the carpets; in their eagerness to be served men in muddy boots leaped upon damask-covered chairs, overturned tables, and brushed bric-à-brac from mantles and walls;" and many received bloody noses in their efforts to obtain refreshments.[81] Even Battle of New Orleans victor President Jackson had to beat a secret and hasty retreat from the White House through the kitchen.[82] Finally the guests were tempted back outside by tubs of punch set out on the lawn.[83]

After Jackson's inauguration, gifts of food poured into the White House — so many that he had trouble storing them. He was given the famed 1,400 pound of cheese, described below, and a number of other huge cheeses; beef from New York; and "a whole hog" was promised from Kentucky. A 700-pound cheese, received in 1837, was finally auctioned off in 1839 for charity by President Van Buren after the White House inhabitants decided not to eat it.[84]

A large crowd attended a reception which Jackson gave in honor of the birth of George Washington in February 1837. At the gala, the noteworthy food item was the huge cheese. N. P. Willis described the scene:

> *"I joined the crowd on the twenty-second of February to pay my respects to the President and see the cheese . . . . On the side of the hall hung a rough likeness of the General emblazoned with eagle and stars, forming a background to the huge tub in which the cheese had been packed; and in the centre of the vestibule stood the 'fragrant gift,' surrounded with a dense crowd, who had, in two hours, eaten, purveyed away fourteen hundred pounds. . . . [B]y four o'clock the guests were gone, and the banquet hall was deserted. Not to leave a wrong impression of the cheese, I dined afterwards at a table to which the President had sent a piece of it, and found it of excellent quality."* [85]

Another writer said:

> *"It was served up in the salle-à-manger, and the whole atmosphere of every room, and throughout the city was filled with the odor. We have met it at every turn — the halls of the Capitol have been perfumed with it, from the members who partook of it having carried away great masses in their coat-pockets."* [86]

Emily Donelson (wife of Rachel's nephew) and Sarah Yorke Jackson (wife of Andrew and Rachel's adopted son) acted as his hostesses.[87] The entertaining was hospitable, yet refined — with the exceptions of the cheese party and inauguration. Jessie Benton (later Fremont), daughter of Senator Thomas Hart Benton, described one of the "great supper parties" which she attended when she was quite young:

"President Jackson at first had suppers at the general receptions, but these had to be given up. He had them, however, for his invited receptions of a thousand or more. It was his wish that I should come to one of these great supper-parties, and I have the beautiful recollection of the whole stately house adorned and ready for the company — (for I was taken early and sent home after a very short stay) — the great wood fires in every room, the immense number of wax-lights softly burning, the stands of camelias [sic] and laurestina [sic] banked row upon row, the glossy dark green leaves bringing into full relief their lovely wax-like flowers; after going all through this silent waiting fairyland, we were taken to the State Dining-Room, where was the gorgeous supper-table shaped like a horseshoe, and covered with every good and glittering thing French skill could devise, and at either end was a monster salmon in waves of meat jelly." [88]

Though Jackson's personal choices in food included his favorite buckwheat-cornmeal flapjacks (pancakes) with hot molasses or buttered maple syrup for breakfast,[89] more complex foods and menus were offered when entertaining. The French chef who had served during John Q. Adams administration was retained by President Jackson.[90] One guest who dined at the White House during the Jackson administration later wrote of being served soup; beef bouille; wild turkey ("boned and dressed with brains"); fish; cold chicken, interlaid with slices of tongue; salad; canvasback duck and celery; partridges with sweet breads; pheasants; and "old Virginia ham,"[91] and numerous desserts; fruits; and wines.[92]

Jackson's kitchen staff could have followed these instructions:

Partridges

"Split down back. Season on both sides with black and red pepper and salt. Have pan hot, drop in plenty of butter; place birds breast down in pan. Cook a nice brown, turn and brown on other side. Pour in one cup boiling water to side, quickly put top on pan and steam four minutes. Cook altogether fifteen minutes." [93]

Mallard Ducks or Canvasback Ducks Roasted
Canards Français ou Canard Cheval Rôtis

1 Pair of Wild Ducks.
1 Tablespoonful Butter [melted, plus additional butter].
Salt and Pepper to Taste.

"Clean the ducks as you would a chicken, without scalding, however. Rinse out the inside and wipe well inside and out with a wet towel. But do not wash the duck unless you have broken the gall bladder, as the washing destroys their flavor. Rub the inside well with salt and pepper, and rub outside as thoroughly. Place a three-inch lump of butter on the inside. Truss nicely and place the ducks in a baking pan, and brush the tops with melted butter. Pour over two tablespoonfuls of water, and set in a very hot oven, and allow them to bake twenty minutes, if they are not very large, and thirty minutes, if larger than the ordinary size of Canvasback Ducks. A wild duck is never cooked dry. It must just reach the point where the blood will not run if the flesh is pierced with the fork in carving. When done, place the ducks in a very hot dish, and serve with their own gravy poured over them. Garnish nicely with parsley or water cress. Serve with Currant Jelly. Always have the plates very hot in which you serve the ducks at table." [94]

Van Buren Administration
March 4, 1837 - March 3, 1841

Martin Van Buren, who was Andrew Jackson's protegé, did not agree with Jackson's open-armed White House hospitality. New York-born Van Buren made social life in the President's House quite exclusive. Gone were the morning receptions and weekly levees. The masses no longer had access to the White House. Van Buren, a widower, cut the large-scale entertaining down to one formal levee per year for the public. This event occurred on New Year's Day. At this and other state occasions no refreshments whatsoever were served.

President Van Buren did enjoy hosting small private dinner parties at the White House at which was served the choicest of food and wine. Most of Van Buren's presidential predecessors did not accept dinner invitations, nor most other social invitations, because acceptance or declining of an invitation might give offense to someone. Van Buren, however, broke with tradition and attended entertainments given by members of his cabinet.[95]

Van Buren, with his four unmarried adult sons, lived most elegantly in the president's home. He directed a thorough cleaning, renovation, and refurnishing of the White House. He tried to improve the heating situation by putting a glass screen across the windy entrance hall, and burning great fires in a "struggle against the chill of the house." Still, the White House experienced drainage problems, and the kitchen and cellar areas stood under water whenever long periods of rain occurred.[96]

Van Buren brought to the White House an English chef, who produced "good and elegant" dinners.[97] Van Buren's table was set with glass, china, silverware, gold forks and knives, and silver plates and serving pieces "that surpassed anything that has been seen in this country."[98] During the financial panic of the late 1830's, opposing political forces spread stories that Van Buren was a cold and haughty aristocrat who ate from gold spoons,[99] and gave speeches that criticized Van Buren "as if he had committed treason" for having such fancy tableware.[100]

Dolley Madison did a little matchmaking during the Van Buren administration, and in 1838 the President's oldest son and private secretary, Abraham, married Angelica Singleton, Dolley's young cousin. After the wedding, the couple moved to the White House where Angelica served as hostess. The next spring the couple had a belated European honeymoon. Upon returning, Angelica once again was mistress of the White House, and she made the Executive Mansion the "centre of social elegance and gayety [sic]." [101]

During the Van Buren administration, ornamental trees and shrubbery were grown on the White House grounds, and from the garden came "fine Neshanock potatoes, honest drumhead and early York cabbages, white and red sugar and pickle beets, marrowfat peas, carrots, parsnips, &c., &c., with an abundance of the strawberry, dewberry, raspberry, &c." [102]

Refined cuisine such as that demonstrated in the following recipe would have been characteristic of the Van Buren administration:

A Boned Turkey

A large turkey.
Three sixpenny loaves of stale bread.
One pound of fresh butter.
Four eggs.
One bunch of pot-herbs, parsley, thyme, and little onions.
Two bunches of sweet-marjoram.
Two bunches of sweet-basil.
Two nutmegs.
Half an ounce of cloves, pounded fine.
A quarter of an ounce of mace, [pounded fine].
A table-spoonful of salt.
A table-spoonful of pepper.

Skewers, tape, needle, and coarse thread will be wanted.

"Grate the bread, and put the crusts in water to soften. Then break them up small into the pan of crumbled

bread. Cut up a pound of butter into the pan of bread. Rub the herbs to powder, and have two table-spoonfuls of sweet-marjoram and two of sweet basil, or more of each if the turkey is very large. Chop the pot-herbs, and pound the spice, then add the salt and pepper, and mix all the ingredients well together. Beat slightly four eggs, and mix them with the seasoning and bread crums [crumbs].

"After the turkey is drawn, take a sharp knife and, beginning at the wings, carefully separate the flesh from the bone, scraping it down as you go; and avoid tearing or breaking the skin. Next, loosen the flesh from the breast and back, and then from the thighs. It requires great care and patience to do it nicely. When all the flesh is thus loosened, take the turkey by the neck, give it a pull, and the skeleton will come out entire from the flesh, as easily as you draw your hand out of a glove. The flesh will then be a shapeless mass. With a needle and thread mend or sew up any holes that may be found in the skin.

"Take up a handful of the seasoning, squeeze it hard and proceed to stuff the turkey with it, beginning at the wings, next to the body, and then the thighs.

"If you stuff it properly, it will again assume its natural shape. Stuff it very hard. When all the stuffing is in, sew up the breast, and skewer the turkey into its proper form, so that it will look as if it had not been boned.

"Tie it round with tape and bake it three hours or more. Make a gravy of the giblets chopped, and enrich it with some wine and an egg.

"If the turkey is to be eaten cold, drop spoonfuls of red currant jelly all over it, and in the dish round it.

"A large fowl may be boned and stuffed in the same manner." [103]

William Henry Harrison
March 4, 1841 - April 4, 1841

William Henry Harrison served only one month. During his short tenure his daughter-in-law, Mrs. William Henry Harrison, Jr., widow of his eldest son, acted as hostess. (The president's wife, Anna, was to follow her husband to Washington in May. She remained at home in Ohio because she was recuperating from an illness. She never made the trip.)

For a few days after he first took office, Harrison could be seen at the market early of a morning, a basket hung over his arm, carefully selecting food for the White House table. Quickly, though, presidential duties overrode his domestic interests, and he directed his steward to do the marketing.[104] Moreover, crowds had begun to gather to watch the President select groceries. Some of these people also took the opportunity to shove petitions in President Harrison's face.[105]

Harrison caught a cold at his inauguration, then died of pneumonia, apparently contracted after being caught in a shower on a walk to market.[106]

Tyler Administration
April 6, 1841 - March 3, 1845

During the John Tyler administration, one of numerous White House weddings occurred when daughter Elizabeth wed William Waller of Williamsburg, Virginia. Dolley Madison, age 73 and as much a belle as ever, attended the society event, along with cabinet members and foreign ministers.[107]

Eight months after Elizabeth Tyler's wedding, her mother died. Two years later President John Tyler remarried, the first Commander-in-Chief to marry while in office. His marriage to New York socialite and beauty Julia Gardiner, who was 35 years younger than he, created a sensation. Their wedding took place in New York City,[108] and a wedding reception for the couple was held two days later in the White House.

Julia, "the Rose of Long Island," [109] had eight months to serve as mistress of the White House before Tyler's term expired. She wrote her mother, "This winter I intend to do something in the way of entertaining that shall be the admiration and talk of the Washington world." She was true to her word, and Washington society experienced impressive weekly White House levees, formal receptions, and several special functions.

The table in the State Dining Room was extended to seat forty. Diners took four hours to work through six to ten courses served "French style." Five or six wines were served, and after eating, guests moved on to the adjacent parlor (now the Red Room) for coffee. The next activity was dancing in the East Room, where the new "craze," waltzing, was practiced freely on the waxed linen floor cloth.[110]

The Christmas celebration was, of course, jolly. The day began "with Egg Nog;" the dinner table was set "à la Virginia (with) immense hams, rounds of beef, veal, etc.;" and the day "concluded with apple Toddy." [111]

At one of Julia's typical "drawing rooms," she received while seated on an improvised throne surrounded by twelve maids of honor in matching gowns. The "Presidentress" herself wore a headdress "formed of bugles and resembling a crown." [112] Among Washington's elder residents, Julia Tyler's ostentatiousness was commented on, and even laughed at.[113]

Nevertheless, Julia rolled gaily along, planning a grand finale farewell ball for February. (At that time inaugurations took place in March.) Three thousand people attended the lavish White House event. Julia's sister wrote, "The supper table, arranged under my own eye, was superb, and wine and champagne flowed like water — *eight* dozen bottles of champagne were drunk with wine by the *barrel*." [114]

The Tylers retired to Sherwood Forest, the Tyler estate in Virginia. They enjoyed 18 years of married life and produced seven children together (John and his first wife had eight children). John died in 1862, Julia in 1889.

The following recipe, actually a modified transparent pudding in a piecrust, has been prepared for decades in the South. It is a family dessert, which John Tyler's 15 children probably enjoyed.

Tyler Pudding

Combine in a double boiler:

1 1/2 cups granulated sugar
1 cup heavy cream
1 1/2 cups brown sugar
Yolks [of] 4 eggs
3/4 cup of butter

[2 unbaked pie shells]

Cook until thick and add vanilla [1 tsp.] and the well-beaten egg whites. (If it does not get thick enough in the cooking, add a little cornstarch.) Pour into pans which have been lined with rich pastry, and sprinkle with nutmeg. [Some prefer to omit nutmeg and sprinkle on grated coconut for the last 5 minutes of baking.] Bake in a moderate oven until custard is set. [Bake at 450° F. for 10 minutes. Reduce heat and bake at 350° F. for 30 minutes.] [115]

Polk Administration
March 4, 1845 - March 3, 1849

James K. Polk was born in Mecklenburg County, North Carolina. When he was about ten years old his family moved to Tennessee, where he eventually served in that state's House of Representatives, then in the Congress, and later as Governor.

As president of the United States, he and his wife Sarah shunned the glittery gay party life of Washington, preferring a more low-key way of interacting socially. Neither dancing, billiards, nor card-playing was permitted in the Polk White House, and no refreshments were offered at public receptions.[116]

Sarah Polk, who was born near Murfreesboro, Tennessee, was religious in nature, having been educated at a Moravian boarding school in North Carolina. As an adult she was a devout Presbyterian.[117]

Dolley Madison was a "presence" at Polk levees, helping President and Mrs. Polk greet guests in the receiving line. When all the guests had been introduced and the people began to mingle, President Polk often gave Mrs. Madison his arm and they strolled together through the crowded rooms, with Mrs. Polk and others following in their wake.[118]

Mrs. Polk did not seem to mind the attention her husband paid Dolley; she even graciously gave Mrs. Madison her place at the dinner table when Dolley was present. The President himself went to help Dolley from her carriage when she arrived at a stylishly late hour to White House receptions or meals.[119] (In later life, Dolley lived in a home near 1600 Pennsylvania Avenue.[120])

Sarah Polk was described as an admirable housekeeper who brought order to the management of the White House.[121] While the Polks were in residence, gas illumination was provided for the public and living areas of the White House. Mrs. Polk, however, kept the candle-lit chandelier in the reception hall because of its beauty. This proved to be a wise decision, for the first night the gas lights were used at a gala, the gas shut off, plunging the house into darkness, except for that one candle-studded chandelier.[122]

President Polk also ordered a furnace and duct system for the main floors of the White House, and authorized other heating improvements, making the home very comfortable by 1846 standards (but still chilly according to the modern norm.)[123] It was during the Polk residency that the White House got its first "refregerator" at a cost of $25.[124]

The Polks' cook came to Washington from Tennessee with them. She prepared the family meals. Auguste Julien, son of Thomas Jefferson's chef, came in especially to prepare the banquets. The Polks personally preferred simple foods, but for dinner parties the service was all "in the French style and each dish a separate course." A Mrs. Dixon guessed that there were 150 different courses at one meal she attended:

"Soup, fish, green peas, spinach, canvas back [sic] duck, turkey, birds, oyster pies, cotolettes di mouton [cocquelets de mouton], ham deliciously garnished, potatoes like snowballs, croquettes poulet, in various forms [see following recipe], duck and olives, patie [sic] foie gras, jellies orange and lemon, charlotte Russe, ices and 'pink mud' oranges, prunes, sweetmeats, mottos [mousses?], and everything one can imagine, all served in silver dishes with silver tureens and wine coolers and the famous gold forks, knives and spoons for dessert." [125]

Cream Croquettes

1 pint chopped chicken or 2 large sweet-breads
1/2 pint milk
Any seasoning preferred
1 large tablespoon butter
2 large tablespoons flour
Lard to fry
Cracker dust to roll in
Salt, pepper, and cayenne to taste

*"**To Make:** Chop the meat very fine; if sweet-breads are used they should be carefully prepared according to directions; put the milk on the fire in a double boiler; rub the flour and butter together; beat until very light; thicken the milk with the butter and flour . . . and stir constantly after thickening until a smooth, thick paste is formed; cook until this leaves the sides of the pan; take it from the fire, and mix the meat thoroughly into the thickened milk; season and turn out to cool; before turning out[,] taste to see if properly seasoned; when*

*cold and firm, form into croquettes; beat the whole egg
until the white and yolk is mixed, add a tablespoon of
water to the egg, stir well, and dip each croquette into
the egg, then in fine bread crumbs or cracker dust; fry in
boiling lard in a frying-basket, if you have one; put on
blotting paper in a pan to drain, and serve hot with or
without sauce. Veal may be substituted for chicken or
sweet-bread."* [126]

Despite the necessary elaborate meals, the President had a
stated preference for "a piece of cornbread and boiled ham." [127]
Mrs. Polk rarely ate anything at the fancy dinners because she
became so involved in conversing with guests. She preferred to
discuss politics with the men, rather than engaging in the lighter
social topics discussed by most ladies of that day. [128]

Sarah planned the first Thanksgiving dinner held in the
White House. [129] About this, a reporter wrote: "The President
had some friends to dinner . . . This new idea of a Thanksgiving
in Washington was well observed and gave such general
satisfaction as to lead to the deduction that it will be an annual
custom hereafter." [130]

Taylor Administration
March 5, 1849 - July 9, 1850

Zachary Taylor served only sixteen months. At a Fourth of
July appearance he became ill, and died five days later. During
his presidency, the ex-general's wife Margaret did not serve as
hostess, due primarily to poor health. The couple's married
daughter, Betty Bliss, assumed the role of White House hostess.
The social tempo increased throughout the Taylor
administration, and by the winter of 1849 elegant dinners were
scheduled twice a week; receptions were held on Tuesday and
Friday afternoons and on Friday evenings; and the Marine Band
gave concerts on the White House lawn every Saturday
afternoon.

Zachary Taylor had been born in Virginia, and reared in Kentucky. His wife was from Maryland. Before his presidency the Taylors lived in Louisiana. In all probability, some of the dishes served at the White House reflected the Louisiana Creole culinary influence and others showed the couple's East Coast roots.

Louisiana Shrimp Gumbo

"Two quarts of fresh okra, put in frying pan with a small amount of lard or cooking oil and 2 chopped onions. Fry very slowly, stirring all the time, to prevent sticking to pan or burning, until soft and dark in color. This process keeps the okra from becoming gummy and sticky. Add a sprig of thyme, 2 bay leaves, salt and pepper to taste. Add 1 3/4 quarts of water, 1 1/2 pints shrimps (raw), 2 slices of ham cut into small cubes. Let all simmer slowly for an hour. Adding 1/2 pint of fresh raw oysters about 10 minutes before gumbo is done improves the flavor. Serve by placing a mound of dry cooked rice in soup plate, pour gumbo around it. If desired, add a few ripe tomatoes. This dish can be made with chicken or fresh crab-meat instead of shrimps." [131]

Pheasants are chicken-like game birds, here served in the French-Creole style.

Pheasants A-La-Daub

"Roast two pheasants in the nicest manner — get a deep dish, the size and form of the one you intend to serve the pheasants in — it must be as deep as a tureen; put in savoury jelly about an inch and a half at the bottom; when that is set, and the pheasants cold, lay them on the jelly with their breasts down; fill the dish with jelly up to their backs; take care it is not warm enough to melt the other, and that the birds are not displaced — just before it is to be served, set it a moment

in hot water to loosen it; put the dish on the top, and turn it out carefully." [132]

Washington Dining

Washingtonians could dine in public eateries, but an invitation to a private home seemed more personal, and when that invitation was to a White House dinner party it was considered a high honor. Ever since the days of Abigail Adams, most White House occupants have been concerned about their food budgets,[133] but still felt it necessary to entertain in style. Some evidently just said to themselves, "Hang the expense!"

The quality of the food served in the homes of prosperous Washingtonians was generally good, although in the early 1800's this had evidently not been the case. In 1822 the Russian minister noted, "Washington with its venison, wild turkeys, canvasbacks, oysters, terrapins, etc. furnished better viands than Paris, and only wanted cooks," [134] but by the mid-1800's Jessie Fremont sang the praises of Washington cuisine, remarking that foreign ministers brought their chefs from Europe with them, and that often these chefs remained here when their employers returned to the Continent. Many of these chefs set up catering businesses. They also trained young slaves who were sent by their owners to be taught how to cook. Observed Mrs. Fremont, "In that way a working knowledge of good cookery of the best French school became diffused among numbers of the colored people — and for cookery they have natural aptitude." [135]

Another writer of the day remarked, "There are mysteries in cooking unattainable to any but the elect, and of the elect were the sable priestesses of the Washington kitchens." [136]

Conclusion

Here, at mid-century, this volume ends. White House cuisine was slowly evolving from the older style characteristic of the young republic into the Victorian style. Earlier food storage and preparation methods gave way to new ideas inspired by technology. Seasonings, manner of presentation and service, and menu complexity were changing. A subsequent volume on this topic will cover another fifty years.

Presidents' and First Ladies'
Dates of Birth and Death

George Washington, born February 22, 1732; died December 14, 1799.
Martha Dandridge Washington, born June 21, 1731; died May 22, 1802.

John Adams, born October 30, 1735; died July 4, 1826.
Abigail Smith Adams, born November 11, 1744; died October 28, 1818.

Thomas Jefferson, born April 13, 1743; died July 4, 1826.
Martha Wayles Skelton Jefferson, born Oct. 19, 1748; died Sept. 6, 1782.

James Madison, born March 16, 1751; died June 28, 1836.
Dolley Dandridge Payne Madison, born May 20, 1768; died July 12, 1849.

James Monroe, born April 28, 1758; died July 4, 1831.
Elizabeth Kortright Monroe, born June 30, 1768; died September 23, 1830.

John Quincy Adams, born July 11, 1767; died February 23, 1848.
Louisa Catherine Johnson Adams, born February 12, 1775; died May 14, 1852.

Andrew Jackson born March 15, 1767; died June 8, 1845.
Rachel Donelson Robards Jackson, born June 15, 1767; died December 22, 1828.

Martin Van Buren, born December 5, 1782; died July 24, 1862.
Hannah Hoes Van Buren, born March 8, 1783; died February 5, 1819.

William H. Harrison, born February 9, 1773; died April 4, 1841.
Anna Tuthill Symmes Harrison, born July 25, 1775; died February 25, 1864.

John Tyler, born March 29, 1790; died January 18, 1862.
Letitia Christian Tyler, born November 12, 1790; died September 10, 1842.
Julia Gardiner Tyler, born May 4, 1820; died July 10, 1889.

James Knox Polk, born November 2, 1795; died June 15, 1849.
Sarah Childress Polk, born September 4, 1803; died August 14, 1891.

Zachary Taylor, born November 24, 1784; died July 9, 1850.
Margaret Mackall Smith Taylor, born Sept. 21, 1788; died August 18, 1852.

Notes

1. Anne Hollingsworth Wharton, *Social Life In The Early Republic*, J. B. Lippincott and Company, New York, 1902, p. 44.

2. Alexander H. Stephens, *A Comprehensive and Popular History of the United States*, Gately & Haskell, Baltimore, MD, 1882, p. 370.

3. Wharton, pp. 26, 46, 49.

4. Lila G. A. Woolfall, *Presiding Ladies of the White House*, Bureau of National Literature and Art, Washington, DC, 1902, p. 121.

5. Gilson Willets, *Inside History of the White House*, The Christian Herald, New York, 1908, p. 42.

6. William Seale, *The President's House, Vol. I*, White House Historical Association with the cooperation of the National Geographic Society, Washington, DC, and Harry N. Abrams, Inc., New York, 1986, p. 29-30.

7. Joseph Jackson, *Development of American Architecture: 1783-1830*, David McKay Company, Philadelphia, 1926, p. 139.

8. Willets, p. 34, 42.

9. Jackson, p. 48, 64.

10. Jane and Burt McConnell, *The White House*, Thomas Y. Crowell Co., New York, 1954, p. 11.

11. Natalie Miller, *The Story of the White House*, Children's Press, Chicago, IL, 1966, p. 8.

12. Willets, p. 28.

13. Laura C. Holloway, *The Ladies of the White House; or, In The Home Of The Presidents*, Bradley & Company, Philadelphia, PA, 1880, p. 76, letter from Abigail Adams to her daughter Mrs. Smith.

14. *Ibid.*, p. 76, 77.

15. *Ibid.*, p. 75, letter from Abigail Adams to Mrs. Smith.

16. Esther Singleton, *The Story of the White House, Vol. I*, The McClure Company, New York, 1907, p. 12.

17. Holloway, p. 76.

18. *Ibid.*, p. 80.

19. Ona Griffin Jeffries, *In and Out of the White House*, Wilfred Funk, New York, 1960, p. 32.

20. Willets, p. 100.

21. Federal Writer's Project, Work Progress Administration, *Washington: City and Capital*, American Guide Series: Washington, United States Government Printing Office, Washington, D. C., 1937, p. 303.

22. Betty Boyd Caroli, *Inside the White House*, Abbeville Press, New York, 1994, p. 42.

23. Willets, pp. 31-32.

24. Irwin Hood (Ike) Hoover, Chief Usher, *Forty-Two Years in the White House*, Houghton Mifflin Company, 1934, reprinted by Greenwood Press, Westport, CT, 1962, p. 5.

25. Caroli, p. 42.

26. Seale, *The President's House, Vol. I*, p. 195.

27. Caroli, p. 41.

28. Mary Randolph, *The Virginia Housewife or The Methodical Cook: a facsimile of an authentic early American cookbook*, E. H. Butler & Co., Philadelphia, 1860, reprinted by Dover Publications, Inc., New York, p. 170 (book originally published in 1824).

29. Amelia Simmons, *American Cookery*, Hudson & Goodwin, Hartford, CT, 1796, p. 32.

30. Allen Johnson, *Jefferson and His Colleagues: A Chronicle of the Virginia Dynasty (The Chronicles of America Series, Vol. 15)*, Yale University Press, New Haven, CT, 1921, p. 7.

31. Bess Furman, *White House Profile*, The Bobbs-Merrill Company, Inc., New York, 1951, p. 42, and Margaret Bayard Smith, edited by Gaillard Hunt, *The First Forty Years of Washington Society portrayed by the Family Letters of Mrs. Samuel Harrison Smith*, C. Scribner's Sons, 1906, p. 391.

32. Margaret Bayard Smith, p. 391. Lemaire was called "the purveyor for the household" in Wharton, p. 106.

33. Jeffries, p. 46.

34. Sarah N. Randolph, *The Domestic Life of Thomas Jefferson*, Harper and Brothers, New York, 1871, p. 339, quoting Thomas Jefferson's grandson, Colonel Jefferson Randolph.

35. Lydia L. Gordon, *From Lady Washington to Mrs. Cleveland*, Lee and Shepherd, Boston, MA, 1888, p. 81. Thomas Jefferson, who had "trusted . . . rough estimates in his head" to keep track of his expenses and was "not . . . sufficiently apprised of the outstanding accounts," found, much to his embarrassment, near the end of his administration that he was seven to eight thousand dollars in debt [probably in part due to his alcohol expenses]. — Sarah N. Randolph, p. 399.

36. Johnson, p. 17.

37. Margaret Bayard Smith, pp. 387-388.

38. "Thomas Jefferson," Thomas Jefferson Memorial, http://www.nps.gov/thje/home.htm, April 2003.

39. Miss Leslie, *Miss Leslie's Complete Cookery: Directions for Cookery, In Its Various Branches, Fifty-First Edition, Thoroughly Revised, with Additions*, Henry Carey Baird, Philadelphia, PA, 1853, p. 438.

40. Mary Randolph, p. 140.

41. Margaret Bayard Smith, p. 412.

42. Willets, pp. 127, 357.

43. Jeffries, p. 55.

44. *The Wise Encyclopedia of Cookery*, William H. Wise & Co., Inc., New York, 1948, p. 629.

45. Allen C. Clark, *Life and Letters of Dolly Madison*, W. F. Roberts Company, Washington, DC, 1914, p. 201, quoting from Lieut. Francis Hall, 14th Light Dragoons, *Travels in Canada and The United States in 1816 and 1817*.

46. Holloway, p. 120.

47. Willets, pp. 219-221.

48. Wharton, p. 167.

49. Perry Wolff, *A Tour of the White House with Mrs. John F. Kennedy*, Doubleday & Company, Inc., Garden City, NY, 1962, p. 80.

50. Johnson, p. 229.

51. Judith St. George, *The White House: Cornerstone of a Nation*, G. P. Putman's Sons, New York, 1990, p. 35.

52. Furman, p. 325.

53. Jessie Benton Fremont, *Souvenirs of My Time*, D. Lothrop & Company, Boston, MA, 1887, p. 115.

54. Paul Jennings, *A Colored Man's Reminiscences of James Madison*, George C. Beadle, Brooklyn, NY, 1865, pp. 14, 15.

55. *The Knoxville Cook Book: A Collection of Practical Tested Recipes by Many of The Best Housekeepers Throughout the Entire United States; For the Benefit of the Girls' Department of the Knox County Industrial School, Revised Edition*, S. B. Newman & Co., Knoxville, TN, 1907, p. 30.

56. Eliza Smith, *The Compleat Housewife*, London, 1758, p. 179.

57. *Ibid.*, p. 184.

58. Mary Randolph, pp. 83-84.

59. *Washington: City and Capital*, p. 309.

60. Holloway, pp. 171-172.

61. Wharton, pp. 185-186.

62. *Ibid.*, pp. 186-187.

63. *Ibid.*, pp. 202-207. Lafayette was also entertained by the Adams at the White House before leaving the United States in September 1825 (p. 207).

64. Caroli, p. 140.

65. Jeffries, p. 73-74.

66. Marie Smith, *Entertaining In the White House*, Acropolis Books, Washington, DC, 1967, p. 52.

67. Singleton, p. 106.

68. Miss Leslie, *Miss Leslie's Complete Cookery*, pp. 481-482.

69. *Virginia Cookery Book: Traditional Recipes*, Virginia League of Women Voters, Richmond, VA, 1921, p. 79, recipe submitted by Miss Nellie Leigh Steward, Petersburg, VA.

70. Singleton, p. 20, 23.

71. Emily Edson Briggs, *The Olivia Letters*, The Neale Publishing Co., New York, 1906, p. 173.

72. Singleton, p. 31.

73. *Ibid.*, p. 155.

74. Gordon, p. 129.

75. Wharton, p. 219.

76. Ben Perley Poore, *Perley's Reminiscences of Sixty Years in the National Metropolis, Vol. I*, Hubbard Brothers, Publishers, Philadelphia, PA, 1886, p. 31.

77. Miss Leslie, *Miss Leslie's Complete Cookery*, p. 486.

78. Miss Leslie, *Seventy-Five Receipts for Pastry, Cakes, and Sweetmeats*, 9th edition, revised, Munroe & Francis, Boston, MA, 1836, p. 31.

79. Frank Freidel, *The Presidents of the United States of America*, White House Historical Association, in cooperation with the National Geographic Society, Washington, DC, 1970, p. 21.

80. Holloway, p. 237.

81. Frederic Austin Ogg, *The Reign of Andrew Jackson: A Chronicle of The Frontier in Politics*, Yale University Press, 1919, p. 123, 124.

82. Margaret Brown Klapthor, *The First Ladies Cook Book*, Parents' Magazine Press, New York, 1977, p. 63.

83. Ogg, p. 123, 124.

84. Willets, p.173, 174.

85. *Ibid.*, pp. 328, 329.

86. Singleton,, pp. 216-217.

87. Holloway, p. 270.

88. Fremont, p. 95.

89. Henry Haller, *The White House Family Cookbook*, Random House, New York, 1987, p. 5.

90. David K. E. Bruce, *Revolution To Reconstruction*, Doubleday, Doran & Company, Inc., New York, 1939, p. 269.

91. Seale, *The President's House, Vol. I*, p. 181.

92. Marie Smith, p. 68.

93. *Virginia Cookery Book*, p. 53, recipe submitted by Mrs. Augustine Royal, Richmond, VA.

94. *The Picayune's Creole Cook Book (Second Edition)*, The Picayune, New Orleans, 1901, p. 138.

95. Poore, p. 221.

96. Fremont, p. 93.

97. *Ibid.*, p. 98.

98. Gordon, p. 181 and Wharton, p. 282.

99. James Moran, *Our Presidents: Brief Biographies of Our Chief Magistrates*, The Macmillan Company, New York, 1930, p. 80.

100. Gordon, p. 181.

101. *Ibid.*, p. 181-183.

102. Singleton, p. 244 (a quote from Congressman Charles Ogle, a contemporary of Van Buren).

103. Miss Leslie, *Seventy-Five Receipts*, pp. 100-101.

104. Singleton, p. 272.

105. Seale, *The President's House, Vol. I*, p. 232.

106. Gordon, p. 198.

107. *Ibid.*, p. 205.

108. Willets, pp. 275-276.

109. Mary Ormsbee Whitten, *First First Ladies: 1789-1865*, Hastings House, New York, 1948, p. 321. The nickname comes from a colored lithograph believed to be of Julia, dated 1840, which is titled "the Rose of Long Island."

110. William Seale, Consulting Historian, "The 1993 White House Christmas Ornament" (a small booklet accompanying the ornament), White House Historical Association, 1993.

111. Klapthor, p. 81.

112. Singleton, p. 293.

113. Fremont, pp. 99, 100.

114. Klapthor, p. 81.

115. Collected and Edited by Harriet Ross Colquitt, *The Savannah Cook Book: A Collection of Old Fashioned Receipts From Colonial Kitchens*, Colonial Publishers, Charleston, SC, 1933, p. 118.

116. Willets, p. 132.

117. Gordon, pp. 217, 221.

118. Willets, pp. 305-306.

119. William Seale, *The President's House, Vol. I*, p. 256.

120. Wharton, p. 274.

121. Fremont, p. 103.

122. Marianne Means, *The Woman in the White House*, Random House, New York, 1963, p. 86.

123. William Seale, *The President's House, Vol. I*, p. 268.

124. William Ryan and Desmond Guinness, *The White House: An Architectural History*, McGraw-Hill Book Company, New York, 1990, p. 132.

125. William Seale, *The President's House, Vol. I*, pp. 273-274.

126. Mrs. John W. Cringan, *Instruction in Cooking: with Selected Receipts*, J. L. Hill Printing Company, Richmond, VA, 1895, p.199.

127. William Seale, *The President's House, Vol. I*, p. 273.

128. Klapthor, p. 85.

129. Jane and Burt McConnell, p. 21.

130. Singleton, p. 308.

131. The University of Virginia Hospital League, *The Monticello Cook Book*, Charlottesville, VA, 1931, p. 14, recipe from Mrs. Murray Boocock.

132. Mary Randolph, pp. 151-152.

133. Caroli, p. 41.

134. Junior League of Washington, Thomas Froncek, ed., *An Illustrated History: The City of Washington*, Alfred A. Knopf, New York, 1985, p. 301.

135. Fremont, p. 98.

136. Klapthor, p. 69.